Torque brims with excitement perfect for thrill-seekers of all kinds. Discover daring survival skills, explore uncharted worlds, and marvel at mighty engines and extreme sports. In *Torque* books, anything can happen. Are you ready?

This edition first published in 2024 by Bellwether Media, Inc.

No part of this publication may be reproduced in whole or in part without written permission of the publisher. For information regarding permission, write to Bellwether Media, Inc., Attention: Permissions Department, 6012 Blue Circle Drive, Minnetonka, MN 55343.

Library of Congress Cataloging-in-Publication Data

LC record for V-22 Osprey available at: https://lccn.loc.gov/2023047013

Text copyright © 2024 by Bellwether Media, Inc. TORQUE and associated logos are trademarks and/or registered trademarks of Bellwether Media, Inc.

Editor: Kieran Downs   Designer: Jeffrey Kollock

Printed in the United States of America, North Mankato, MN.

TABLE OF CONTENTS

PLANE OR HELICOPTER?	4
WHAT IS THE V-22 OSPREY?	6
FANCY FLYING	10
THE OSPREY'S FUTURE	18
V-22 OSPREY FACTS	20
GLOSSARY	22
TO LEARN MORE	23
INDEX	24

PLANE OR HELICOPTER?

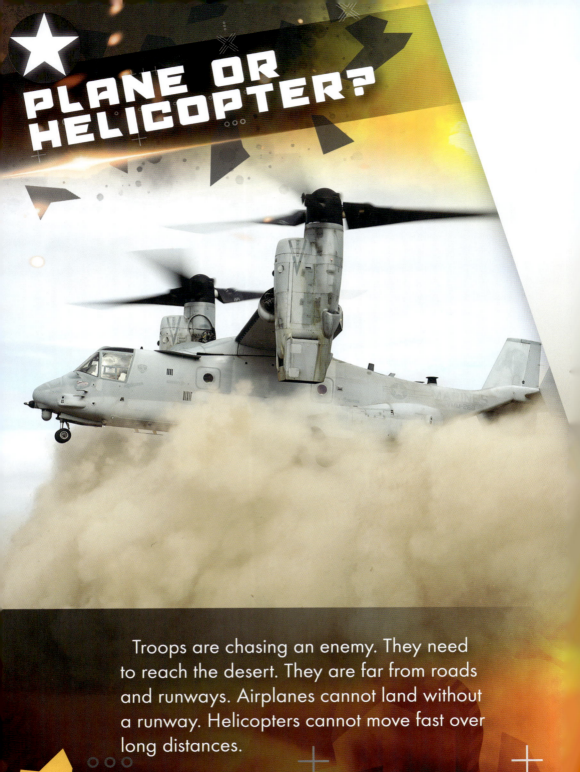

Troops are chasing an enemy. They need to reach the desert. They are far from roads and runways. Airplanes cannot land without a runway. Helicopters cannot move fast over long distances.

The troops fly in the V-22 Osprey. This aircraft can land without a runway. It can quickly move the troops. It safely lands in the desert. The troops can complete their mission!

SPECIAL OPS

Military special operation forces use a special Osprey. It is called the CV-22. It is used in the most difficult, high-risk missions!

WHAT IS THE V-22 OSPREY?

CARGO

The Osprey is a multirole **combat** aircraft. Its main job is to carry troops and **cargo**. It is also used in rescue missions.

SIZE CHART

LENGTH
57.3 FEET (17.5 METERS)

HEIGHT
22 FEET (6.7 METERS)

WIDTH AND WINGSPAN
84.6 FEET (25.8 METERS)

The Osprey was the first aircraft designed to be used by all **branches** of the United States military. Today, three branches use it. They are the Air Force, Marine Corps, and Navy.

The Osprey was first used in 1999. It was first flown by the U.S. Marines. It replaced the CH-46 Sea Knight helicopter. The Osprey first saw combat with the Marines in 2007.

CH-46 SEA KNIGHT

Ospreys were used in 2016. They helped aid Haiti after **Hurricane** Matthew. They carried supplies. They also helped move troops in Iraq in 2020.

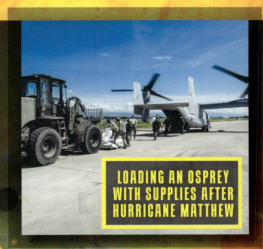

LOADING AN OSPREY WITH SUPPLIES AFTER HURRICANE MATTHEW

MISSIONS MAP

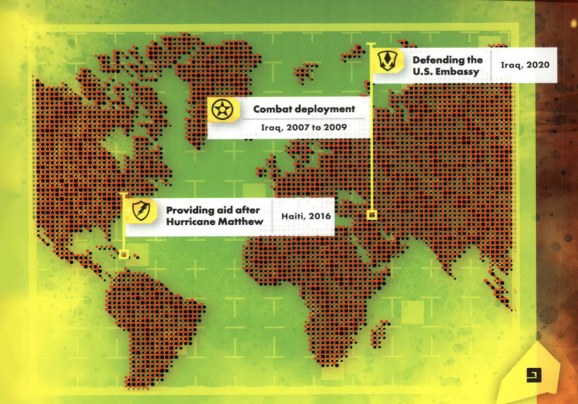

Defending the U.S. Embassy — Iraq, 2020

Combat deployment — Iraq, 2007 to 2009

Providing aid after Hurricane Matthew — Haiti, 2016

FANCY FLYING

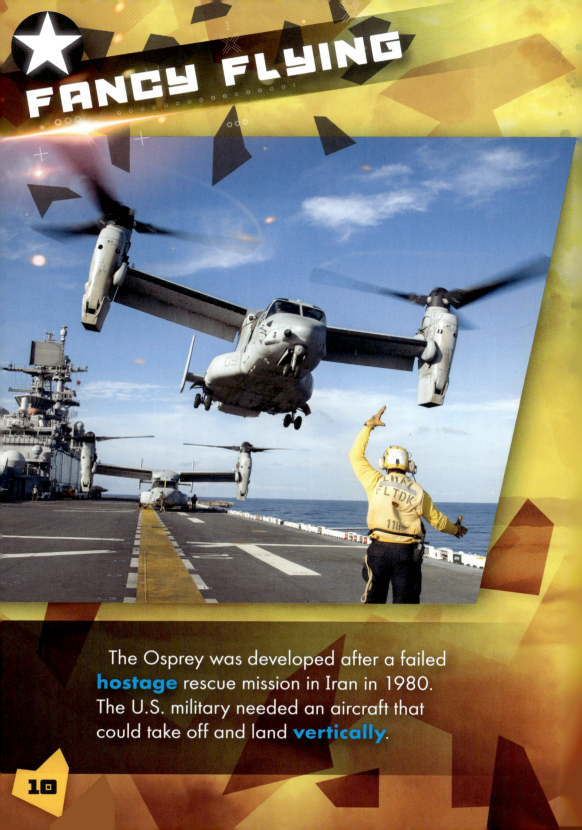

The Osprey was developed after a failed **hostage** rescue mission in Iran in 1980. The U.S. military needed an aircraft that could take off and land **vertically**.

PARTS OF A V-22 OSPREY

- FOLDING WING
- COCKPIT
- LANDING GEAR
- REAR LOADING RAMP
- CABIN FOR 24 TROOPS
- FOLDING ROTOR

The aircraft needed to then travel at high speeds. It also needed to be sturdy in bad weather and dust storms. The Osprey became the U.S. military's first **tilt-rotor** aircraft.

The Osprey takes off and lands like a helicopter. Its rotors twirl like helicopter blades. When it is in the air, its rotors shift. They work like airplane propellers. They can switch in 12 seconds.

HOW TILT-ROTORS WORK

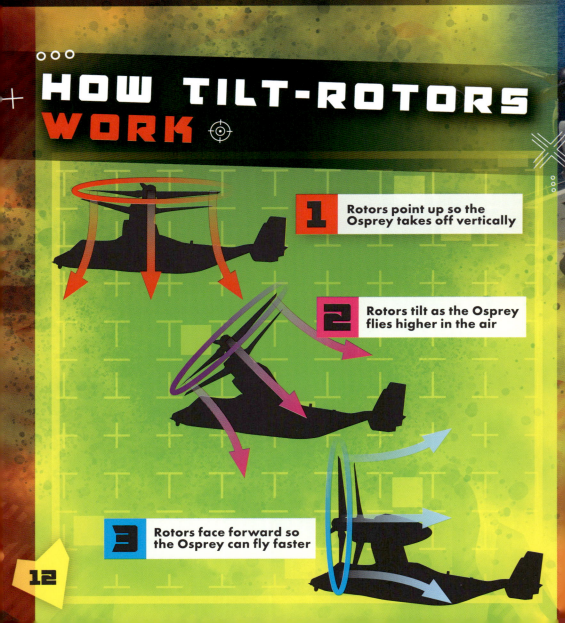

1. Rotors point up so the Osprey takes off vertically
2. Rotors tilt as the Osprey flies higher in the air
3. Rotors face forward so the Osprey can fly faster

FOLDING WINGS

When the Osprey lands on a ship, its wings are folded up. It takes up less space on the ship!

The Osprey can land on ships at sea. It can land in rough areas. It carries out missions that would normally require both a helicopter and an airplane.

The Osprey is equipped for combat. It can be armed with rockets and machine guns. Its guns are found on its belly and at its tail.

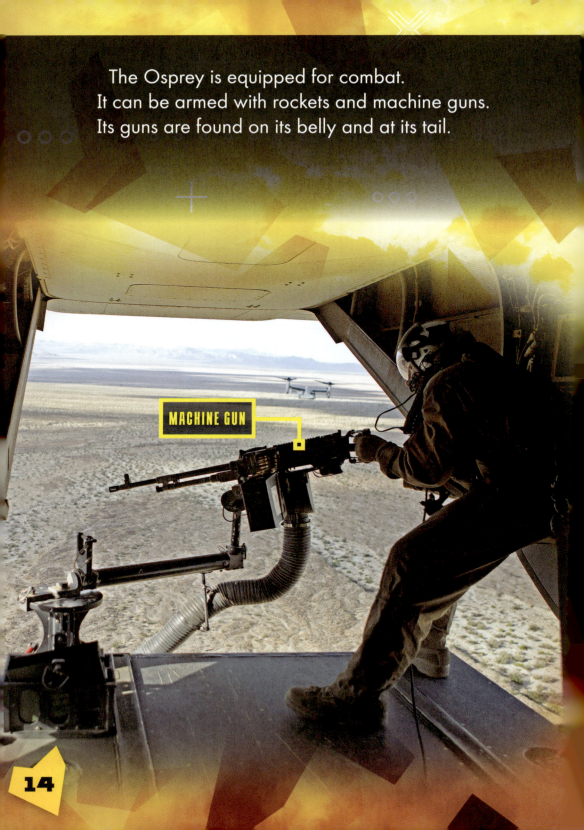

MACHINE GUN

14

The Osprey uses **radar** to help it fly. This helps the pilot fly safely. Special coatings help it fly in tough weather.

CO-PILOT

PILOT

FLIGHT ENGINEER

The Osprey has two crew members. They are a pilot and a co-pilot. Sometimes a **flight engineer** is also part of the crew.

The Osprey can carry up to 24 troops or 20,000 pounds (9,072 kilograms) of cargo. Troops enter and exit the aircraft on a ramp in the cargo area. They can also **parachute** out of the Osprey.

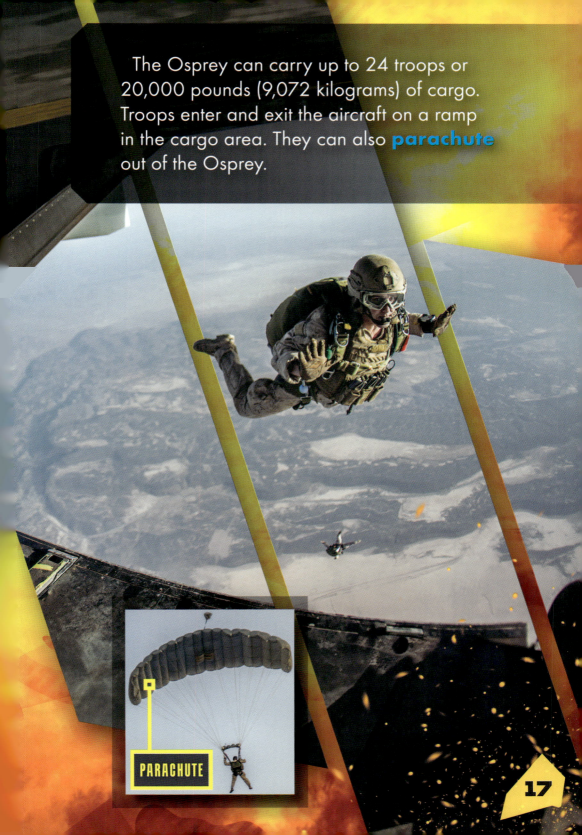

PARACHUTE

THE OSPREY'S FUTURE

The U.S. military has slowed down on building new Ospreys. However, they plan to keep using this unique aircraft through 2055.

Ospreys continue to carry troops and cargo on land and at sea. They conduct search and rescue missions. They move troops in and out of dangerous areas. Ospreys will keep helping the military for years to come!

V-22 OSPREY FACTS

STATS

TOP SPEED

311 miles
(500 kilometers)
per hour

RANGE

575 miles
(925 kilometers)

ALTITUDE CEILING

25,000 feet
(7,620 meters)

WEAPONS

2 ROCKETS

400 400 400 400
400 400 400 400
400 400

4,000 MACHINE GUN ROUNDS

CLASS
TILT-ROTOR AIRCRAFT

CREW
2 OR 3

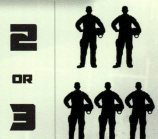

OPERATION

MORE THAN **475** V-22 OSPREYS IN USE TODAY

MANUFACTURERS

Bell-Boeing

BRANCHES OF THE MILITARY

U.S. Air Force

U.S. Marine Corps

U.S. Navy

MAIN PURPOSE

multi-role combat aircraft

FIRST YEAR USED

1999

21

GLOSSARY

branches—divisions of the U.S. military; the branches of the military are the Air Force, Army, Coast Guard, Marines, Navy, and Space Force.

cargo—gear or equipment being moved from one place to another

combat—related to a fight between armed forces

flight engineer—a member of the crew responsible for the aircraft's engines

hostage—relating to a person captured and held by another person or group

hurricane—a storm formed in the tropics that has violent winds and often has rain and lightning

parachute—to land on the ground using a parachute; a parachute is a device made of fabric that catches air to slow a fall.

radar—a device that uses energy waves to sense and see objects

tilt-rotor—related to an aircraft with rotors at the end of each wing that can be moved to different positions; rotors are spinning blades that help an aircraft fly.

vertically—related to moving straight up or down

TO LEARN MORE

AT THE LIBRARY

Brody, Walt. *How Military Helicopters Work*. Minneapolis, Minn.: Lerner Publications, 2020.

McKinney, Donna. *Apache Helicopter*. Minneapolis, Minn.: Bellwether Media, 2024.

Schuh, Mari. *Military Aircraft*. North Mankato, Minn.: Pebble, 2022.

ON THE WEB

FACTSURFER

Factsurfer.com gives you a safe, fun way to find more information.

1. Go to www.factsurfer.com

2. Enter "V-22 Osprey" into the search box and click 🔍.

3. Select your book cover to see a list of related content.

INDEX

branches, 7, 8
cargo, 6, 17, 18
CH-46 Sea Knight, 8
coatings, 15
combat, 6, 8, 14
co-pilot, 16
crew, 16
CV-22, 5
enemies, 4
flight engineer, 16
future, 18
Haiti, 9
history, 8, 9, 10, 11
Iran, 10
Iraq, 9
machine guns, 14
map, 9
missions, 5, 6, 8, 9, 10, 13, 18
parachute, 17
parts of a V-22 Osprey, 11
pilot, 15, 16

radar, 15
ramp, 17
rescue, 6, 10, 18
rockets, 14
rotors, 12
runways, 4, 5
ships, 13
size, 7
speeds, 4, 5, 11
tail, 14
tilt-rotor, 11, 12
troops, 4, 5, 6, 9, 17, 18
United States Air Force, 7
United States Marines Corps, 7, 8
United States Navy, 7
V-22 Osprey facts, 20–21
weapons, 14
weather, 11, 15
wings, 13

The images in this book are reproduced through the courtesy of: BeAvPhoto, cover; Ruben Padilla/ DVIDS, pp. 3, 6 (cargo); Keith Anderson/ DVIDS, p. 4; Garrett White/ DVIDS, p. 5; Dangelo Yanez/ DVIDS, p. 6; Adam Wainwright/ DVIDS, p. 8 (Sea Knight); Mark Andries/ DVIDS, pp. 8, 20; Robert Waggoner/ DVIDS, p. 9; Peter Burghart/ DVIDS, p. 10; Saniparp Wattanaporn, p. 11 (front); BlueBarronPhoto, p. 11 (back); Isaac Lamberth/ DVIDS, p. 13 (fun fact); Christian Salazar/ DVIDS, p. 13; Becky Cleveland/ DVIDS, p. 14; Jason Allred/ DVIDS, p. 15; Joseph Pick/ DVIDS, p. 16; Chris Stone/ DVIDS, p. 17; Desire Mora/ DVIDS, p. 17 (parachute); Emeline Molla/ DVIDS, p. 18; Jessica Avallone/ DVIDS, p. 19; VanderWolf Images, p. 23.